GLAD I DON'T LOOK LIKE WHAT I HAVE BEEN THROUGH

Gloria F. (Hatley) Sanders

ISBN 978-1-0980-9973-2 (paperback)
ISBN 978-1-0980-9974-9 (digital)

Christian Faith Publishing
832 Park Avenue
Meadville, PA 16335
www.christianfaithpublishing.com

Printed in the United States of America

Author's Note

Hello, my name is Gloria F. Sanders. I am a native of Dallas, Texas. I now reside in Lansing, Michigan, for the last sixty-one years. I have serious testimonies I want to share with you all from my heart. This is my story, and this is my song. I praise my savior all day long. *This is my story.* I have never been so ready to share my amazing story. Thank you for allowing me to tell you my story. Because you don't know it, I want to share it with you all. I really don't know where to start, so I think I will just jump right in. I've had some good days, and I've had some hills to climb. I have had some weary days and oh so many sleepless nights. But when I look around and think things over, all of my good days outweigh my bad days, so I won't complain. I pray there is something in my book that will encourage and inspire you to keep on keeping on. We have to know we are more than conquerors through Christ Jesus, who strengthens us. Be and stay blessed as you read my story. Please read to the end.

This started in October or November of 2006. I had a colonoscopy, and they discovered that I had a polyp. They removed it, and I was told by Dr. Katheleen Kershen, Lake Lansing Road, that the polyp was nothing to worry about. Then she told me to come back for a repeat in five years, in 2011. However, 2008 threw a different light on my situation. On November 18, 2008, I was diagnosed with colon cancer, stage 3, and couldn't understand how that could have happened since there was no sign of it when I had the colonoscopy in 2006. Had it not been for the Lord on my side, I would not be here today. Thank you, Jesus, for helping me overcome my illness before it's too late. Dr. Daniel Coffey removed a 5.3 tumor from the cena part of my colon, twelve inches to be exact.

Why did I go through what I went through? Why? I often ask myself, *why these things happened to me. Not sure; however, since they did, My God is getting all of the Glory from this story.*

Not only was I diagnosed with stage three colon cancer on November 18 but on March of 2009, I was diagnosed with small cell lung cancer, which resulted in me having my right lung lobe removed by Dr. Gary Roth at Ingham Medical on April 20, 2009, with complete recovery. My lung cancer hadn't gotten to any stage. It did not metastasize. Both were primary, and my doctor said it was better for both to be primary and not metastasized; although none was better to me at all. I was too angry. I really believed that Dr. D. M. and her staff in another city injected the cancer cell into me when I was there getting checked for my adrenal gland, which she has been keeping watch on for me for about six years.

Something took a terrible turn, resulting in being diagnosed with two cancers in four months. *Lord, why, why, why?*

Lord, I am glad that I don't look like what I have been through. Praise God's holy name. Thank you, *Jesus.*

On December 11, 2008, I had a hemicolectomy by Dr. Daniel Coffey. I was in the hospital at Sparrow Hospital, 1215 E. Michigan Ave. Michigan Ave Campus, for eleven days. I healed as best as I could until April 20, 2009, when I had lung surgery by Dr. Gary Roth at Ingham Medical. I was in there for eight days. Both surgeries took a toll on me without me realizing for a long time, As I look back, I can see how it was extremely difficult. Thank you, Jesus, for being with me every step of the way.

Then I started a six-month bout with heavy chemotherapy. I would go golfing on Tuesdays and on Wednesdays I would go and get hooked up to chemo. My friend Barbara Boos, who took me there or met me there every single time, except just one time when she just couldn't because her daughter was in town and needed some help. I got extremely sick about two times during the whole six-month ordeal. I got hooked up on Wednesday, and the chemo would run continually, on Wednesday, Thursday, and Friday noon. I would go back to get disconnected. Then I would be good until the next treatment. I finished those terrible treatments on November 18, 2009. On August 23, 2013, I was cancer *free*. Praise God. My PET scan taken in July 2013 was excellent. Thank you, King Jesus.

This ride had been one of the worst times in my entire life. I praised God all the way through this. He was with me then and still with me. I continually praise God, and as of October 2, 2013, Wednesday, I was still cancer free. Thank you, Jesus.

I knew someone missed that tumor in my colon—Dr. Katheleen Kershen. She did my colonoscopy and said there was nothing there. However, a nurse at Dr. Jaffer's office said the report from 2006 plainly said it was a precancer, so why wasn't I told that and why didn't she contact me after getting the report? I believed I had a malpractice suit there, but I was not sure how to proceed with it.

When I was going through this terrible time in my life, I was really never afraid, and I know it had to be because Jesus was by my side all the way, as he promised he would be—never leaving me nor forsaking me. He is the King of kings and the Lord of Lords. He healed me, and I truly thank him. I want to spend the rest of my life telling people about the goodness of Jesus Christ and all he has done for me. God is just so good.

This cancerous word stands over my head every time and all the time. I have got to throw it out of my head and my mind so I can continue to live my life to the fullest. Every time I get a sore or a sore throat or different things, I would think, *Oh no, it's back.* When it comes back in my head and mind, I must begin and continue to say, *No weapon formed against me shall prosper.*

I was in my mother's doctor's office, and she told my mom her white blood cells were down at 10.2. My report revealed that my white blood cells were down at 9.6. I knew I had to be in trouble, so I immediately called my doctor, Dr. Barbara Saxena, to get it checked out. She sent me to get a test that revealed cancer seemed to be present. What I meant to say was, I never totally believe a doctor and their reports. Had I tried to wait for my scheduled appointment in 2011, I would have been dead. But praise be to God, I am still here in spite of my situation.

I know wholeheartedly that Dr. Kerchen missed my diagnosis and almost cost me my life. I was still very angry for what happened to me. I was trying not to be angry, but it was oh so hard not to be. I am sure you would be angry too.

It was Friday, October 25, 2013. I was almost five years in remission. My colon surgery was on December 11, 2008. My lung surgery was on April 20, 2009. My primary care physician said that out of all the years she has been in her practice, she has never ever heard of a person to have two primary cancers so close together. I asked her if they could have made a mistake with two primaries and if it was really metastasized instead of being just primary. Dr. Roth said it is best to have two primaries than one that spread. I felt like there were many people who have gotten wrong diagnosis.

At this point in my life, I am still very, very angry and asking how it happened. But to God be the glory, my testimony is I am still here and feeling good. Sometimes it feels like it never really happened. However, I know it did. Sometimes I wonder how on God's earth did I make it this far without having reoccurrences. Then I'd say, "Through no one else but God."

At one point in my life, I thought a doctor had injected the cancer virus into my body for some kind of research reason, which I would consider very unprofessional—*who does that* besides someone who thinks to themselves, *I will have to treat them with chemo or radiation, for that would be very profitable for me?* That chemo that I had cost approximately $120,000. My, my, my, medicine is so extremely expensive. But God is just so good, and he is good all the time. I said to myself, *Let not your heart be troubled. Believe in God. Believe also in me. Because in my Father's house are many mansions. If it were not so, he would have told me.* I also thought about Isaiah 53:5 that says, "By God's stripes, I am already healed." In Jesus's name. And my cancer will never return again. Never ever. In Jesus's name. I will bless the Lord at all times, and his praises shall continuously be in my mouth. Hallelujah and amen. Thank you, Jesus, for healing me totally. Blessed be the name of the Lord. I love you, Jesus, because you first loved me. Thank you for that.

I went from the diagnosis to my complete healing from December 11, 2008, to November 2009. I've had three PET scans, and they were all excellent. Praise God. I planned on getting another great report on January 2014. I had my last one on July 18, 2013, which was very good except my CEA level was really high at 6.4. I have never had it that high before. When I was first diagnosed, it was 3.4, and it had been fluctuating ever since—3.4, 4.1, 3.8. They said it could rise from smoking and other different things. But I don't smoke. So I had to wait and see what would happen the next time. *To God be the glory* for all that he has done in my life. Thank you, Jesus. You are great and worthy to be praised. Blessed be the name of the Lord.

When I first got diagnosed, it really turned my world completely upside down. I didn't know what to do or how to do it. I was completely shocked and upset and angry, and at this point, I was still *angry*. I tried to let it go. I just couldn't do it yet. Also, I haven't spoken with anyone about this disease. I have never said, out of my mouth, that I was a survivor of two major cancers. And thanks be to God I was still here five years later on December 7, 2013, Sunday. Thank you, Jesus. You are just so good, and you are good all the time.

I know my survival wasn't just for me. It was also for those people who would benefit to hear my testimony, which they probably would not believe. I heard Bishop T. D. Jakes say something like "God will heal and bless you so good that people won't believe your testimony." I hope, trust, and pray they will believe my testimony. Really, my testimony is *I am still here*.

I can also say I am so, so glad I don't look like what I have been through. Thank you, Jesus. It was December 8, 2013, Sunday. Because I have been through some very difficult times within the last five years, I was giving God all the praise, glory, and honor. God was right by my side all the way. And I thank him so much for saving my life and giving me strength and courage to climb the mountain. He did not move the mountain, but he did give me strength. It was nothing but a blessing from the Almighty God. I came through both major surgeries with flying colors. No problems during surgery or after my cancer battle. I did lose my complete appetite for about three to four days. Scary but thanks be to our God, my appetite returned, and I've never had any problems since—another blessing from the King of kings and the Lord of lords.

Isn't the Lord good? Sitting here this Wednesday, December 12, 2014, 8:45 p.m. Thanking God for all he has done, is doing, and all he is going to do. *Thank you, Jesus.*

God left me here for such a time as this. I hate to think how my sweet mom would have made it through this difficult time she went through from January 31, 2014, to this very present moment, Monday, April 7, 2014. She got where she couldn't stand up, my friend, Barbara Boos, went over to my mom's house. I had moved to Hawaii because staying in Lansing had become too stressful for me. I felt so disconnected to my daughter, my grandchildren, and my family. What do you do when there is no connection between you and your family, whom you love so much?

It is Monday, April 7, 2014. What I am saying is, how could someone think there is no God? He healed me of a double death sentence. Only a God like my God can do such a thing. I am truly grateful and appreciative for his great love for me. Had it not been for the Lord on my side, where would I be.

I still feel really bad sometimes. If a sore or pain develops on me, it always feels like my mind is trying to tell me my disease has returned. That I know is not true because no weapon formed against me is going to prosper; it might form, but it will not prosper. That is God's word for me. I am hanging on to God's promises to me. It is written—by God's stripes, we are already healed. In Jesus's name, I thank God for my healing.

I am really interested in how cancer starts in a person's body. Is it caused by something they eat or drink, or is it caused by the environment they are in? I have heard that every person has cancer cells in them. It just needs something to set them off. It seemed like we could figure this out. I hate that I am still angry this day, April 28, 2014. I asked God to continue to lead, guide, and direct everything I do.

Cancer is a very strange disease. However, I did everything I was supposed to do. Today's date is July 30, 2014, and I am still *angry*—rightfully so, I believe. This should have never happened to me. I heard Meryl Streep say catching colon cancer is very easy to do. I know without a shadow of a doubt that Dr. Katheleen Kershen missed a precancer polyp that almost cost me my life. But God kept me in spite of the missed, false report. I am still not able to talk about what happened to me because it is so painful and I am not comfortable talking about it. Meryl said if you do your colonoscopy like you should, you can always catch a polyp before it becomes a huge tumor, like the one they took out of me. I could scream to the very top of my voice because it hurt so bad. I never ever had a symptom of any kind indicating I had cancer. How I detected it was, I took my mom to her doctor's appointment, Dr. Carol Rapson, and my mom's hemoglobin was at 10.5. The doctor said her hemoglobin was low, and I had just read my CBC, and my hemoglobin was 9.5. Red light, bells, and everything went on. I made an appointment to see my primary care physician, Dr. Barbara Saxena, then she gave me a test to see if there was blood in my feces, and yes, there was. That was in November of 2008. Then a colonoscopy was ordered from Dr. Jaffer. A large tumor was detected. Dr. Coffey did my surgery on December 11, 2008, at Sparrow Hospital. I was in the hospital until December 22, 2008, for eleven days. I knew I was very ill, especially when you stay in a hospital that long. Oh but God, oh but God, he took me through it. Nothing shy of a miracle. Praise God. Sharonda, Sade, Khadija, and Asia came to get me and brought me home. It was super cold outside. They picked me up in Shawn's white

Cadillac. We picked my prescription up, came home, took a hot shower, washed my hair, and went to bed after I ate a turkey sandwich and soup. They left, and I went to bed. It was a very long journey, lots of tests and trials, but God, oh but God, he healed me then in 2008 and he continues to heal me and keep me strong until today, August 13, 2014. Thank you, King Jesus, thank you, Heavenly Father.

You don't know my story. You don't know the things I've been through. I've been through the trying times of my illnesses and very trying times with my one and only child—she didn't care for me enough to help me through this. I did not have her support at all. It seemed like she could have been a little more compassionate toward me, knowing what I was going through then and now. But she was so distant from me, and she was teaching my grandchildren to also treat me bad. I really didn't appreciate her doing that, but they were doing what they saw her do. She may have helped this disease to materialize in my body. We haven't gotten along for a long time. Oh but my God, God is still on the throne, and I know he is not coming down. What had been the hardest for me was not having the love and support from my one and only daughter that I love so much, but she doesn't feel the same toward me. But I was so happy I was standing up to cancer. I have beaten it. Thank God. Thank you, Jesus. Hallelujah and amen.

I was looking at a program called Stand Up to Cancer (SU2C) standuptocancer.org. 1-888-907-8263-9-5-14, saying we have beaten cancer but that we want to do more. Thank God for my wonderful healing. If I had ten thousand tongues, I would praise him, with every one of them, and that wouldn't be enough. I couldn't thank God enough. Thank you, Jesus. God has blessed me with an extended beautiful life, given me a second chance at this life; now I am able to help other people. That is a blessing from our God. Thank you, Jesus. I could have died, but I came out fighting. God never told us it would be easy, but he did tell us, "Whatever you go through, I will go through it with you." What a blessed assurance. Thanks be to God I am cancer free, working on my sixth year this October 11, 2014, Saturday. What a wonderful God we serve. I am a walking miracle. Thank you, Jesus.

Every time I hear someone say, "I have cancer," I want to be able to say, "I had it twice within four months. *I made it, and you can too.* I had two cancers, and they were not related. They said that it was better for them to be primary than to be spreading. But

God just continually blessed and kept me as only he can do. Where do I go from here? Only God knows."

Now that I am cancer free, every time I get a sore or a sore throat or a bruise, I think the worse. I run into so many people who has been diagnosed with this dreadful disease. I want to be able to give other people hope, as I am almost six years in remission. Praise our wonderful God.

I have never been able to talk about what happened to me, I have only been able to talk to two or three people regarding my health issues. I did tell my daughter, and I asked her not to talk with other people about it, but come to find out, she has told other people, especially my grandchildren. I knew this because one day, I had both of my grandchildren in the car and my sister Mattie was with us. My granddaughter Khadija shouted from the back seat saying, "Granny, did you know you are a cancer survivor?"

I said to her, "Who told you that?"

She said, "My mom."

I said, "Your mom does not know what she is talking about," because it hurt me so bad that she would discuss it with people when I had clearly asked her not to talk about it. My sister Mattie acted like that was the first time she had heard that, but I know better than that. I did tell her a little white lie, an untruth, because I was just not ready to talk about it, plus I was writing a best seller, and I don't want to spill the beans and give away the book's story because then, no one will buy the book. But this story needs to be told. It has to be told. Maybe this book can help someone else along the way, to let them know that God healed me, and he can do the same for them if they only believe.

When a doctor tells you, "You have cancer," it absolutely turns your world upside down, round and around. You really don't know which way is up. I do believe by me not telling people helped me to survive. Many of my friends and associates that were diagnosed when I was, sadly did not survive and went to be with the Lord. Each one of them are in heaven telling the story of how they made it over. To many people around you when you are going through, it sometimes drains you of your energy when you talk about anything concerning your cancer; I know sometimes it helps, but in my case, I decided to keep it between me and God and the few people I said it to.

November 19, 2014: Sometimes I want to tell people about my nightmare. But I would always think, *No, don't say nothing. You are going to spoil this best seller.* This was how I know that God wants me to tell other people my story because so many people will benefit from it. God has just been so good to me, and I know he wants me to tell my testimony. You never have a testimony without a *test*. I most certainly have had my share of tests and trials. But thanks be to God, for he has been with me every step of the way. I am very appreciative. I just want to stop and say, "Father God, help me to magnify your goodness and mercy as I tell people how you blessed me, healed me, and kept me from going completely out of my mind."

God kept me. He let me feel no fear at all, I wasn't fearful going into surgery, coming out of surgery, and at no time did I fear when I was going through this. I never feared—*that had to be God.* Sweeping things under the rug doesn't change things. I didn't want to talk about it, think about it—nothing about it. The time will come when I will deal with it. I am sure this is not healthy for me or anyone else. Running from your health issues can waste a lot of time. Don't run from things. We should be facing them head on. If you don't learn from your past, you will repeat them. We must put our trust in God. When you don't understand as I did, you must put your trust in the almighty God and keep your eyes on the prize. After you go through situations as I did, get up, dust yourself off, and help others get through as you did. Where do I go from here? God is still on the throne, and I know he will lead, guide, and direct me. I want to get this book out in the atmosphere.

January 26, 2015—this story has to be told. It has to be. Plus, I want all to know cancer is not always a death sentence. Had it not been for *God* on my side, I would not be here today. Some say when this diagnosis is delivered to you, it all has a different life span. A lot depends on how healthy the person is in the very beginning of the onset of the illness. Attitude plays a big part in your healing. I just thank *God* that he has been with me every step of the way, up until this very day, Thursday, January 29, 2015. God is still on his throne, and I will bless his name at all times and his praises will continually be in my mouth. Praise God.

When you have a sore or something pop up creeping into your head, trying to make you think about it more than you should, and try to make you think about it could be trying to make another ugly appearance. But God is on the throne. No weapon formed against me, against us, shall prosper. We have been healed by God's stripes. That is what the word of God says, and I certainly believe it. I am so happy I don't look like what I have been through. Thank you, King Jesus. I have been through my share of trials and tribulations, but through it all, I have learned to trust in Jesus. I have learned to trust in God—through it all. Sometimes I wonder how I got over. My soul looks back and wonder how I made it over. "Amazing grace, how sweet the sound that saved a wretch like me. I once was lost, but now, I am found, was blind but now I see." Thanks be to God for all of his indescribable gifts. When I was going through my trials and tribulations, I continuously said in my spirit, "I shall live and not die and proclaim God's glory" (Psalm 118:17). "Even when we were dead in our sins, God made us alive together with him" (Ephesians 2:5).

Psalm 119:24 says, "Your testimonies also are my delight and my counselors." This was why I know that I must tell this heart-wrenching story. Maybe it is not heart-wrenching to you, but it certainly is to me. I have never, in all the days of my life, ever heard of a story like this one. I am sure the stories are out there. All I can say to God is, thank you, God, for saving my life and letting me be able to live and to tell of God's amazing healing power. It is still very amazing how God did this for me.

A two-time cancer survivor and I am now six years out, with no reoccurring issues concerning the cancer. December 15, 2015, Sunday. God is just so good. I will stand on top of the highest mountain and shout it out all over the world—what the Lord did for me, a little country girl from Dallas, Texas. If he did it for me, he can do it for you and anyone else that believes, in all of his heart and soul, that God is a divine healer, comforter, miracle worker. Oh yes, he is still working miracles in all of our lives.

My grandson, LaDarion, recently went through his miracle of surviving an almost fatal accident. He ran into the back of a hummer with a small neon. He got a big, big bump on the left side of his head that caused him a slight brain damage. He was in intensive care for eleven days. He went into the hospital on August 17 and got out on September 5. He was supposed to get discharged on September 10, but my God worked another one of his miracles on my grandson. He keeps on doing great things for me and my family. Thank you, Jesus. You are an awesome, wonderful God. What shall I render for all God has done for me? I will continue praising God for all of his miracle-working powers. He is an all-powerful God, with all kinds of miracles.

March 11, 2015, Wednesday. I really hope, trust, and pray that one of these days, my daughter will realize how much better I could do if I had her support and compassion to help me through this very difficult time in my life, where it seemed like my life was almost over. But I believe with all of my heart that my daughter helped this disease to manifest itself in my body because of the stress created—because of the way she ignores me, of how she never calls me or do so only when she wants something.

I love, love, my daughter so much, but I am certainly getting tired of the way my daughter treats me. I just really want her to leave me alone, and I will do likewise for her. She really treats me awful. I love her so much, and with love and kindness have I tried to draw her, but it is not working. There comes a time in a person's life where they have to let go. I love her, but I don't like her at all. I love her, but I see she does not love me. When we are at church, I would come to the point where I want to go up in the balcony and stay away from her. I didn't want any of her fake hugs and "I love yous." All of it is fake, fake, fake. I would do better if she would just stay away from me, just as I am going to do that for her. But I believe she will need me before I need her. I really and truly can't believe how she treats me. I have heard people say people treat you the way you let them treat you; well, I am sick and tired of it. She knows what I have been through. It is like she really doesn't care. No one knows how this feels. I wrote a letter to my daughter, telling her we are wasting a lot of precious time not spending time with each other and that I wanted to get together to walk, talk, have lunch or dinner, movies, or do something together; but she doesn't want to, so I needed to leave her alone and let her go ahead and do her own thing while I do my own thing. I feel like she is driving me bonkers. I have got to let her go. It hurts so bad—so, so bad. However, I know God will see me through this one also. If he can heal me from the two cancers, I am sure he can take care of this hurt I am feeling. Please, Jesus, I need your help.

This is what I want people to take from this book—life is not always what it looks like on the outside and that God can do anything but fail. I have often thought about getting a surrogate daughter to do things with me and to love me as a daughter should. I was never so shocked, in all the days of my entire life, to hear these devastating words being said unto me, "YOU HAVE CANCER". It was like they were saying, if you got a bucket list, you better get about your business trying to do it. It seemed like my life was turned completely upside down, round and around. You never realize how that can cause you to almost throw in the towel and go crazy. It was like they were saying, "Your life is over"—but God. As I said before, I never felt afraid until years later. But God is still on the throne and taking care of me. He told me in his Word that he would never leave me nor forsake me. God is keeping me and my mind. God is a very present help in times of trouble. What could I render or say because of this terrible, terrible ordeal? How can I help my brother and sister to get through their trial? I do say, if I can come through this, then so can you. We are more than conquerors. I am sitting here at this moment while I am cruising on the Norwegian getaway cruise ship. It is June 14, 2015. I am thanking and praising God for all he has done, is doing, and is going to do. The weather is just beautiful—salty seawater misting over the deck. Every time I hear of someone telling my story, I always cringe because I am not telling my story, and then I hear so many sharing my story, and they do it with so much ease. I am sure I will get to that point someday and someway with God's help.

As I think about it, it's closer for me than I can ever imagine. I know God is going to be so pleased because all of this is going to glorify him, and this is exactly what I want it to do, and I praise God for all things.

Sometimes when I hear other people say, "I've got cancer," or "I am going through chemo and radiation," or "I just finished my chemo," I want to tell them, "You can make it. I did, six and a half years ago. And if he did it for me, he can do the same for you. Just have and keep the faith and ask God for what you want. If you want healing for your body, he said in his word, if two or three of us ask anything in his name, he would hear and give it to us. God is not a man that he should lie. He says what he means and means what he says. He also said in his word that by his stripes, we are already healed. I feel at this moment that I am totally healed and the disease will never ever return to this body—not now, not ever." Thank you, Jesus. Hallelujah and amen.

Jesus continues to take very good care of me. Just before my cruise, maybe two weeks before, the devil tried to attack my body with some extremely bad pain on my left side. I took my temperature. It was June 3, right after golf, and my temperature was 100.2 degrees for two or three times. Then it went down to 99.9 and then to 98.9, then 98.5. I didn't understand why. The pain was unbearable. I was going to go to urgent care. However, since my temperature started going down, I decided to shower and go to bed.

June 16, 2015, Tuesday. I felt like I had a death sentence hung over me the day they said, "Yes, you have cancer." As I said before, I never felt scared since then till now. Sometimes when I think there is a possibility or a chance that this dreadful disease would come back, it would frighten me at first, but all of a sudden, I would hear God saying, "Fear not for I am with you. God's rod and staff comfort me."

I say to God, "You are my rod and shield, a very present help in the time of trouble" (Psalm 46:1). When I am in trouble, I call on none other than Jesus Christ, the son of the living God, because he is the only one that can do anything about my situation. I try not to run to God with stuff I can do for myself, but so many times, I have no choice but to call on the name of the Lord. When I call him, he always answers—morning, noon, or night. He is a very present help in the time of trouble, and I so thank him for all of his indescribable gifts unto me and my family and friends.

Who, what, why, when, where are the questions I need to concentrate on asking as I continue to give God the glory for every good thing he is doing.

What should I have learned from this dreadful thing that happened to me? However, I know that no weapon formed against me shall prosper at all. Things will form, but they will not prosper. I just thank God things are as well off as they are. It is truly a blessing, I had that dreadful disease and have never ever had a reoccurrence in these last seven years (today's date is July 17, 2015). Thank you, Jesus. Hallelujah and amen. When I give God all the honor, praise, and glory, he continues to keep me as only he can. I remember in his word he said that if you will keep your mind staying on him, he will keep us in perfect peace (Isaiah 26:3). Thank you, Jesus, because it would be hard to stay in peace if you did not have Jesus in your life/heart. Thank you, Jesus for keeping me healthy so that I can continue on helping my sweet mom to keep living a beautiful, productive life. (I know God saved me for such a time as this to help with the care of my ninety-three-year-old mom.)

December 1, 2015. Taking care of my mom is certainly not an easy task, and it is getting more challenging as the days go on. As my mom gets younger, it is getting extremely challenging. I am not sure how much longer I can do it. I am getting to the end of my rope. I heard someone say that when you think you are at the end of your rope, tie a knot in it and hang on in there; that is what I am doing. I think that assisted living quarters is nearer than we think. I am hurting my body and my mind in trying to keep everything afloat. I even hurt my shoulder trying to help mom out of my house; it was too much weight on my shoulder.

December 14, 2015, Monday. In 2008, I was sentenced to death (*but God*) twice in my life, on December 11, 2008, and April 20, 2009. Having had two major surgeries within four months of each other was not easy. In 2008, I had a hemicolectomy—that is, part of my bowels was removed, twelve inches to be exact. I stayed in the hospital for eleven days. In 2009, I had a lobe on my right lung removed and was in the hospital for one week. I almost lost my life. I just thank the Almighty God for keeping me up to this very present moment, keeping me safe, happy, healthy, and enjoying life. This has really been an uphill journey. (But God.) He has always been with me through it all. That's why I know that through anything I go through, he will be right there for me to lean on. Thank you, Jesus. Hallelujah.

December 15, 2015. I had an episode on Sunday, December 13, 2015, at the church. Our pastor, Dr. Walter Gibson, asked which members of the congregation have ever had cancer and are still here after one/two/three/four/five/six/seven years. It was the very first time I have ever acknowledged I was a survivor. I have never been able to talk about it or acknowledge it. I was not sure if I would be able to converse concerning what happened to me. It still felt very uncomfortable, but I could see it was going to get easier because I realized this situation of mine, if told or discussed, could truly help other people who are going through that same thing. They would really benefit, and they would be more encouraged knowing I went through it, and I really didn't feel like I looked sick. Praise God. I will continue to praise God for the rest of my days. God takes care of us, and I thank him. Hallelujah and amen.

There was a lady at our church, and I could tell she would benefit from knowing I made it through. But I was just not ready to talk about it. It still didn't feel right. It felt right in a way, and in another way, it didn't. But I realized this story needed to be told soon. I wanted this book to inspire people with similar situations, to know that if I did it, then they can also do it. Since God is for us, no one and no disease can be against us or conquer us or even dampen our spirits. God is still a very present help in the time of trouble. As I have said before, when I run into trouble, I run straight to God, and he is always there for me. Thank you, Lord Jesus.

I heard two of my friends tell their testimony at a Christmas luncheon, stating how they had been at death's doors, and it seemed they spoke of their illness with no hesitation and freely explained what happened to them. It was something I felt I never could have done that, but I could tell I was going to get to that point where I, too, will feel as they did; maybe yes and maybe no—because no two people feel the same in a situation. Maybe I could say, "I wished I felt the way they did and could expose or talk on it with no regrets or hesitation."

I really wish I could talk on it freely. I do believe that day is coming soon. This is why I must finish this book very soon. Today's date is December 21, 2015. I hope to have this book finished within the next year or two. With God's help and my determination, we can do it.

I would love to take a survey or poll on how many people handle their sickness and illness like I have. I am sure I am not the only person who feels uncomfortable discussing their sickness. Oh yeah, what do you think when you ask your very closest relative not to discuss your illness with anyone, only to come find out that they have told several people about it? I think it is *rude* and not good. I would not have done that to them if they told me not to discuss it with others. I felt very betrayed by their action.

December 24, 2015, Thursday. God wants our experiences to help others, and I am so ready to help as many people as I can. I can let them know it was hard, but I made it through by the grace of

God. And I thank God every day, all day. My situation is really like an "Amazing Grace" story. I sing Hallelujah and amen, hallelujah and amen, all the time. I do have something to praise God for. This was absolutely a miracle. I know it, and anybody that reads my story will echo me—nothing but a miracle. I will be extremely, eternally grateful for all he has done for me. Thank you, Heavenly Father, for keeping me for seven years on this journey. Hallelujah and praise God's holy name. Sometimes I still wonder what these trials and tribulations were for. However, it has taught me to value every single moment of my life because tomorrow is not promised to us. So what I have decided to do is live each day like it is my very last day on this earth. You appreciate life more dearly after you have survived two death sentences thrown at you, one right after the other. Praise God's holy name. He is so good. He is the great healer, and I am a living witness and want to tell it all over the world. Thank you, Heavenly Father, for your mercy and your grace, your loving-kindness, your blessings. What shall I render for all that the Lord has done for me?

It certainly has to be a God. No one else could heal you of the lung and colon diseases I had seven years ago. He has kept me healthy with no reoccurrences whatsoever. Praise God's holy name. God, I know you are real. I didn't just find that out seven years ago. I've seen God's miracles all through my life. Starting from my conception to this very moment, 9:50 p.m., Christmas Eve. December 24, 2015. God, you are an awesome God, not just for what you do in my life. I see you working in lots of my associates' lives as well. You are just a wonderful God. You are the Lord of lords and the King of kings, and you are most worthy to be praised. God has healed me so well. They are not going to believe my testimony—I am sharing with you all. Praise God is all I can say. This is all I need to say. *Praise God.*

January 18, 2016. I realized, at this stage in my life, that as soon as healing takes place, we are to go out and heal somebody else. We must get it out to those in need, pull someone else along with you. I realized I can be a valuable tool in someone's healing process. But because of my inability to communicate this to others, I am not helping others have hope, in a way that would give others a lot of hope, they would say. "If she did it, so can I." I am working more intensely and harder on my book because I am anxious to get it out. It will give many hope and inspiration. So I am asking God to give me the most appropriate way to tell my story. I know someone will say, "I can't believe it." Some will say, "What a miracle. What a miracle." Then others will say, "I thought she looked extremely sick for a while there."

As I look back on pictures of myself during my recovery, I thought I looked pretty good for what I went through. Sometimes it is so good that you don't look like what you are going through. That is a plus. I can say on some of the pictures, I looked extremely dark, that had to be that chemo, but God kept me looking pretty good, kept my spirits up, kept me from thinking, *Woe is me*. God continues to keep me. Praise God. He kept me as I continued this dreary journey. Some did not make it, but I am still here. As I said before, I live each day as if it is my last day. I enjoy each day. Thank you, King Jesus. Thank you, Jesus, for keeping my mind staying on you. I couldn't have made it this far had it not been for our Heavenly Father Jesus Christ. I will continue to keep the faith and stay on Jesus's team, no matter what.

Thank you, Jesus, for a great day this February 1, 2016. What I think of is I had a tussle with the devil but I won. Thank you, Jesus. I feel like I am better now than I was before. Praise your name, Jesus. I know there is a frame built around my life, body, and soul, believing the words we speak are very powerful, as I journey down this road of surgery, healing, and getting my life somewhat back on track. I kept my mind staying on Jesus Christ. I did not speak negatively about what was going on in my life when I went through my chemotherapy. I never stopped doing the things I always did. I played golf every week and did my laundry, my housecleaning, and the things I needed to do for my mom. I was still sociable as usual. I was a little tired but not so much.

Sunday, June 11, 2017. Now that my daughter is experiencing this same kind of treatment, I feel so sorry for her because it is not going to be an easy job. I know she can make it, just like I did. I will be there for her every step of the way, if that is what she wants. I ask Father God to help me tell this story where it will glorify him and him alone. I don't won't to struggle with telling this amazing story. I have got to tell it. I can't keep it anymore. I know in my heart of hearts God wants me to tell this story and show the world what can be done with an impossible-looking situation, and my situation looked very impossible. When God is in control, nothing is impossible with God. What is impossible with men is possible with God.

Thank you, Jesus. God continues to bless me beyond measures, over and over again. I am an amazing grace—that I know. I don't take for granted what God has done for me. I just continue to praise God all the day long. God is so good, and he is good all the time. Great is his faithfulness. Lord, unto thee. I thank God for his indescribable gifts unto me. Here I am cruising the great North Atlantic in Saint John, New Brunswick. The ship is docked, and I am chillaxing and trying to finish my book. I know it is going to be a blessing to many, to my family and friends, and even to people I do not know will be encouraged and say, as they go through a similar journey, "I can do this with God's help."

I don't think a person can make it without our God on their side. Because going through something like this is a very tough and trying time. It tests your faith continually at all points as you continue to go through the trials and tribulations. It is rough and tough, no doubt. When we keep Jesus on our side, our road is not going to be impossible. God is going to be with us through it all. At least he was there for me every single step of the way. I praise God for all he has done, is doing, and I know he will continue to keep me. What shall I render to the Lord for all he has done for me? All I can say is, "Thank you, Jesus. Jesus, you are awesome."

Back to my daughter, Sharonda. I feel like she is afraid but she kind of doesn't want to admit it. And again, maybe she truly is not afraid for me or her. There is really not a reason to be afraid. God has already told us many times, "Fear not for I am with you. And I will never ever leave you or forsake you." The Word also says that when you feel fear, that is not of the Lord because "the Lord has not given us a spirit of fear but of love, power, and a sound mind."

One thing we also know is the word *fear* means *f*alse *e*vidence *a*ppearing *r*eal. I have just got to believe that in my life, I will never ever be fearful again. Never. If I wasn't fearful with the life-threatening illnesses I had, then there is no reason to fear. I have been through the storm and the rain, the worst part of my entire life—a part of my life I wouldn't wish on my enemy. I really believe they have found a cure for cancer and just don't won't to let the world know because it would cost the pharmaceutical, medical people. It would cost them billions of dollars because for everyone that is diagnosed with cancer, their treatment is going to cost them one hundred fifty to two hundred thousand dollars. Look how much money will be taken from the medical part. They do not want to lose money like that. So they say there is no cure. I really believe they can cure it. It would probably cost them fifty to seventy-five thousand to cure it. But with chemo, the medicine would cost twice the amount for the medicine. Every time I turn around these days, someone else has cancer.

Sometimes I think cancer is contagious—very much so. I asked a doctor and they said, "No, it is not contagious. You can't catch it."

Then I said, "Well, since they don't know, it is a possibility it can be caught."

So while I was going through it, I always wore gloves when I was cooking for other people, just in case it could be caught. I just played it safe and gloved up. I still glove up. It has become a habit. Now I just really wear gloves any time I am cooking. I still don't know what happened to me, what caused this dreadful disease to attach itself to me. Who is the cause of this happening to me? My doctor, Katheleen Kershen.

June 14, 2017. I just can't stop being angry. I am angry, angry, angry, and I can't help it. I am asking the Lord to help me get over this anger. I know he is going to help me. At least I hope so. He told me in his Word that where two or three are gathered in his name, there he would be, right there in the midst. He also said we could ask anything we wanted to ask and it would be given to us if we had faith the size of a mustard seed, so I am asking and believing in my heart that he will take this anger from me. I certainly hope, trust, and pray that I won't be angry any longer because me being angry is not helping anyone, especially me.

December 23, 2017. I am on a cruise for the holidays, cruising on the *Koningsdam*, Holland America Line. I have never been on this line, but I believe they have won me over. I am liking it a lot. So watch out Royal Caribbean, Norwegian, and Carnival because Holland America is showing me some altogether different things. They paid my gratuities, prepaid hotel charge of $13.95 per day, which is $94.50 total, plus gave me a $25.00 beverage card. None of the other lines has ever done anything like that for me. So thank you again, Jesus, for your indescribable gifts. For the last couple or three weeks, I have been experiencing a sore right breast. They say there is nothing there, but it feels very sore and heavy. I will have an ultrasound upon returning home. I am praising God that it will not be anything. Jesus said in his Word to speak those things that are not as though they are.

Where do I go from here? I want to hurry and get this best seller out there. Knowing I am going to be helping so many on their journey. Yesterday would have been the ninth year of survival of my colon surgery. I came home from that terrible eleven-day stay in the hospital, Sparrow Hospital. I went in December 11 for that colon surgery and got out on December 22 of 2008. I Praise God I am still here to tell you about it. Praise God's holy name. Not everyone was fortunate as I am. I know people that were diagnosed with just one cancer, and they went on to heaven to be with our Heavenly Father. Evidently God had more plans for me. My journey was not completed. I believe one reason I am still here was God wanted me to take care of my nine-ty-five-year-old mother. God bless her beautiful soul. She is a trooper, showing us what serving God can do for us. I am a living witness of what he will do for us. Hallelujah and amen. Thank you, Jesus. After I survived the colon cancer in 2008, I was diagnosed with small cell lung cancer. I said to myself, *How much more can I take?* It was not metastatic. It was primary. My primary physician said she has not ever seen two primaries so close to each other without them being metastatic. Praise God for healing me from both of them. Thank you, Jesus. Thank you, Jesus.

December 22, 2019, Sunday. Basically the bottom line is trust in God. I am a living witness that he will come through for you if you just trust him. Put your trust in Jesus. Put your trust in no man because man will defile you, but God never will. I love you, Lord. You heard my cry and pitied my every groan many times. Thank you, Heavenly Father. Today,

Dec. 22, 2019, I am on the *Rotterdam* cruise ship. I am thanking and praising God for all he has done for me. Now I have been experiencing swollen sinus that blocks my smell and taste. Nothing brings my smell back and stops my sinuses from swelling but steroids, methylprednisolone, four-milligram dose pack. I have been working with several ENT doctors, one in Lansing and one in University Plaza, Ann Arbor. I have been going to her since September 30, 2019, with no help whatsoever. First, she said I am allergic to mold and told me to take Allegra every day, do sinus rinse, and prednisolone spray up my nostril daily, which did not help at all. So I called her and told her I wanted to go on this cruise, but if she could prescribe some steroid or give me a letter then I could withdraw from this seventeen-day cruise. Her nurse, Sarah, called me back and said Dr. Blank would not write a script for steroids, and she said, "She is not going to write a letter for you to get your money back because not being able to smell or taste is not debilitating." She, however, said that if I have an allergist or pulmonary doctor, I could call and see if they would write a script for me. I don't have an allergist, never saw one. I have been seeing the ENT in Ann Arbor. She was the one that said I was allergic to mold. So when I get back, she will not be my ENT any longer for sure.

I then tried to get an environmental person to check if the mold is lurking around in my house, in the basement or somewhere. I did have some water leak in my house during the storm of 2013 that perhaps did not get completely dry. Anyhow I went to my primary care physician and she wrote me a prescription for the steroids that worked marvelously. I started taking the steroids on Friday, December 20; I did not have smell or taste yet. Usually on the first day I take them, my smell comes back, but it hasn't yet, so I continued taking them on Saturday, December 21, where I got on my flight at 6:21 a.m., still with no smell but with little taste. When something like this happens to you, you can't help but think, *Is this a cancer in my sinuses?* I could see swelling in my sinus from the MRI, but something was still in my head. Is this cancer? All I could say is OMG.

I woke up Sunday morning, December 22, 2019, at 10:00 a.m., with my smell and taste completely back, and food was tasting very good. I couldn't stop praising God all day long. Thank you, King Jesus. No one in their right mind wants to be on a seventeen-day cruise and can't smell or taste. Sarah, the nurse for the ENT doctor in Ann Arbor, said she would go anyway, even if she couldn't smell or taste; that was probably because she has never been on a cruise. Didn't she know that being on a cruise without your smell and taste is torture? Smell and taste go with cruising. I thank God for my primary—that made all the difference in the world for me to enjoy my cruise. That other doctor is not going to be my doctor anymore. What she was doing for me wasn't working. I am going to another doctor in East Lansing when I get back home; hopefully he can help. I just really want to know what causes the swelling in my sinuses that blocks my smell and taste. I am asking King Jesus to help us to find out what is the origin of this happening to me. It is very scary. I am trying not to be fearful. Jesus, please help. I am calling on you for your mercy and grace. My primary care physician said the dose is a very low dose. All I know is it does the trick almost instantly. This time, it took a little longer than before, and maybe the reason for the slow action now compared to that time in July 13, 2019 is there was no antibiotics involved. We will get to the bottom of this. I am praying without ceasing. As I said, my thoughts turned to, *Is cancer trying to raise its ugly head up in my sinuses and smelling cavities?* Then I said to myself, *No weapon formed against me will prosper. They will form, but they will not prosper.* Then I said to myself, *This is just a trick of the devil trying to make me be fearful.* But I keep hearing God say, "Fear not because I am with you, like I have been with you all the other times." He said, "I have not given you a spirit of fear but of love, power, and sound mind." I did say to myself, *If it is cancer, no steroids could take it away the way the steroids do.* That gives me comfort in knowing something is strange. I don't know what is happening, but I know my God knows what is happening, and he has the power to do something about it. I started praising God early this morning. It is now 5:00 p.m., and I am still getting my praise on. I am going to continue praising him until I find out what is happening. My nose doesn't feel stuffed. My ears don't feel too stuffy. My smell and my taste are back, 96 percent of the way. I know the 4 percent is on its way, in a hurry. Thank you, Jesus.

The bottom line is: God is an awesome God, healing and keeping and delivering people each and every day. No one can make me doubt him because I know too much about him. Blessed be the name of the Almighty God. He is the King of kings and the Lord of lords. I am going to trust him until the day I die. He has been too good to me, and I will tell it on top of any mountain. He has been with me from the rocking of my cradle until this very precious moment., Thursday, December 26, 2019. I am sure he will be with me on the rest of my journey. Thanking him in advance. Thank you, Jesus. What shall I render for all of the love and kindness he has done for me? *I will bless the Lord all of the rest of my life.* We bless you and your name forever. I am so glad you loved and love me, and I love you. We will be together forever. Lord, help me to witness to people about you with effectiveness. I want it to be clear what I am saying to them. The message is get Jesus in your life. If you have him in your life—*great.* If you don't have him in your life, I am urging you to ask Jesus to come into your life. Things are always better when Jesus is your friend. I repeat—when Jesus is your friend, things are much better. I have tried both ways. I haven't been saved all of my little life. But now, I know I am on the winning team. No doubt. I am still trying to figure out how some people can live without Jesus. Jesus, Jesus, how could they? I always say to some, "I love God. You don't love God. What is wrong with you?" If you don't love God, I think there is something wrong with you. I just don't understand. I can't understand for the life of me.

As I was about to make my closing statement, I thought to myself. I must tell them of another death sentence/miracle that God worked in my life. This death sentence tried to come and test my faith, AGAIN. But thanks be to my God, He brought me out of an open heart bypass surgery. (Quadruple). There are people that say there is no God. But if there is no God, who brought me through all of these death sentence. Open heart bypass surgery is a special surgery. Nobody can bring you out of something like a quadruple open heart bypass surgery but my GOD.

Thank you, Jesus. I couldn't have made it through this last one without my God. All I can say is Jesus takes care of his own, and I am his own. I am a living and walking testimony. I never would have thought in my wildest dream that I would have four blocked arteries. And I have been going to a cardiologist for the last four years. I have taken stress test three times to be exact. Echocardiograms three times also and the doctor did not see anything abnormal. As I try to read up on blocked arteries, they are saying one of the test should have told him, something is not right here. So we finally did a heart scan. It showed I had three blocked arteries. On the left, my main artery was 100 percent blocked. The two on my right, one was 99 percent blocked and the other one was 98 percent blocked. Who has that much blockage and don't have a heart attack, stroke, or something. But my God was taking care of me like he has always. I am so thankful that I made it through. The cardiologist said I had three blocked arteries, but when the surgeon finished the surgery and came in to see me he said, "you thought you had three blocked arteries. No, you had four totally blocked arteries."

Oh my God! Yes, I am a living and walking testimony. I couldn't have made it without the Lord. No way. I am nine months out of surgery. The surgery was not easy but God did it again. I am very grateful and thankful that God saw fit to let me live a while longer. Thank you, Jesus. I can't stop praising God and I am not going to stop not now not never. I will tell my testimony until I die.

I hope to be warmly remembered by everyone that know me.

In my closing—Jesus has always been a very present help for me in my time of trouble, trials, and tribulation. Now I have had my share of trials and tribulations, many that I never mentioned. I can't complain because Jesus has always been right there for me through it all. As the songwriter said, "Through it all, I have learned to trust in Jesus. I have learned to trust in God. *Through it all.*" Thank you, Jesus. I have had some good days. I have had some *bad days.* I have had many hills to climb, but truly my good days have outweighed my bad days, so I am not going to complain. As I look around, there are so many people who are much worse off than myself, so I won't complain. In the beginning, I told you I had some miracles that you wouldn't believe; but now, I hope, trust, and pray that you believe me. So take me at my word—God will be with us all if we just trust and believe in him.

Thank you for allowing me to tell you my story. I hope it will help you in some small ways because everyone goes through things. So if you have to go through some things, just be encouraged; you can make it, like I have made it.

Bottom line: Totally put your trust in our Lord and Savior, Jesus Christ. He is the only one you can totally depend on.

Please believe me.

In Christ Jesus,
Gloria, aka GG

About the Author

The author is Gloria F. (Hatley) Sanders. She was born in Dallas, Texas, at Parkland Hospital on June 15, 1949. She had five siblings. She went to school in Lansing, Michigan. She dropped out of school two years before it was time for her to graduate; however, she went back to school and graduated in 1981 in a class of six hundred eighty-five students; the oldest person that graduated with her was eighty-six years old. She graduated from Harry Hill High School in Lansing, received her GED, and was very proud to accomplish this. Afterward, she went to Lansing Community College for a degree in business administration. She worked for General Motors for thirty-eight years. She started working for them in 1969 and retired in 2007. She is currently retired. She loves reading her Bible, practicing piano, walking and riding her bicycle for exercise. She tries to do all the good she can for whom she can while she can.

www.ingramcontent.com/pod-product-compliance
Lightning Source LLC
Chambersburg PA
CBHW031544060726
47590CB00004BA/1503